POPULAR
SONGS
HAL LEONARD
STUDENT PIANO LIBRARY

Pop Hits
for Piano Duet

Arranged by Jeremy Siskind

T0081802

ISBN 978-1-4950-9034-9

HAL•LEONARD®
7777 W. BLUEMOUND RD. P.O. BOX 13819 MILWAUKEE, WI 53213

Visit Hal Leonard Online at
www.halleonard.com

From the Arranger

A wise person once said that there are two types of music: music to make you sing, and music to make you dance. This collection of duets is all about making you dance! These funky tunes, Motown hits, and swaying ballads were all chosen to get your body moving, whether the material comes from soul legends like Stevie Wonder and Ray Charles or from modern hit makers like Bruno Mars and Beyoncé. Feel free to tap your foot, or bob your head, or "shake your groove thang" with the music while you jam on these hits with your partner.

Enjoy!

Pianist **Jeremy Siskind** is the winner of the 2012 Nottingham International Jazz Piano Competition and the second place winner of the 2011 Montreux Solo Piano Competition. A two-time finalist for the American Pianist Association's Cole Porter Fellowship, Siskind has performed jazz and classical music at Carnegie Hall, the Kennedy Center, in Japan, Switzerland, Thailand, Cyprus, England, Lebanon, India, Tunisia, France, and China. Siskind served as the chair of the Keyboard Area at Western Michigan University until 2017, when he joined the piano faculty of Fullerton College in Southern California. Siskind is also a leader of the house concert movement, having performed in over 100 houses in 24 different states around the U.S., and given presentations on in-home concerts at Jazz Education Network, MTNA, and Chamber Music America conferences.

A proud Yamaha Artist since 2013, he holds degrees from the Eastman School of Music (Jazz Performance and Music Theory) and Columbia University (English and Comparative Literature). His teachers include Tamir Hendelman, Tony Caramia, Harold Danko, Rose Grace, Sophia Rosoff, and Fred Hersch.

CONTENTS

Can't Feel My Face

Words and Music by Abel Tesfaye,
Max Martin, Savan Kotecha,
Peter Svensson and Ali Payami
Arranged by Jeremy Siskind

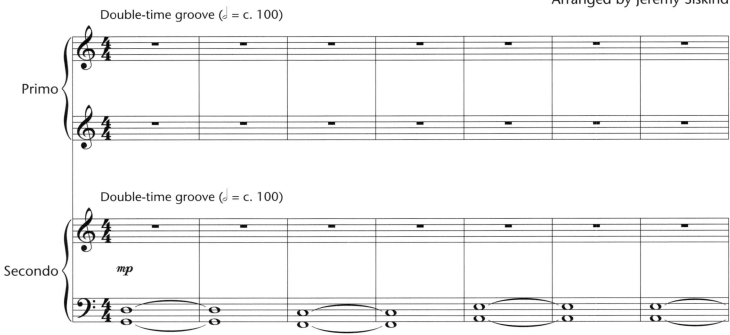

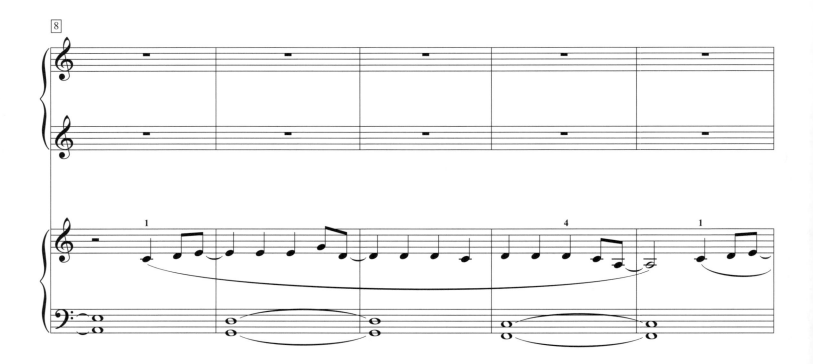

5

11

Hallelujah, I Love Her So

Words and Music by
Ray Charles
Arranged by Jeremy Siskind

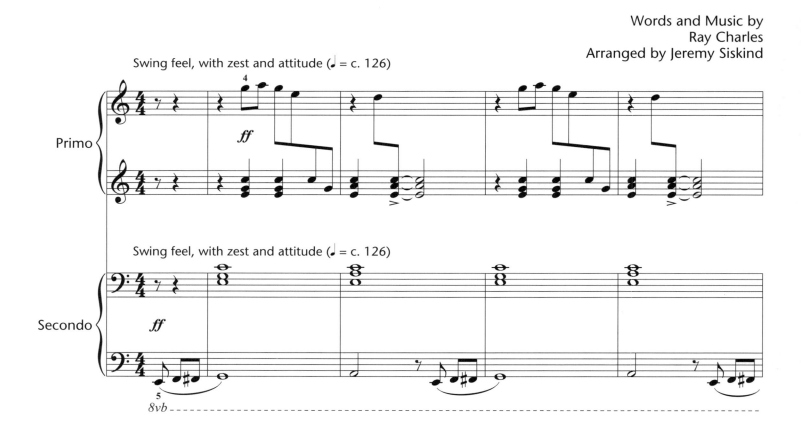

Halo

Words and Music by Beyoncé Knowles,
Ryan Tedder and Evan Bogart
Arranged by Jeremy Siskind

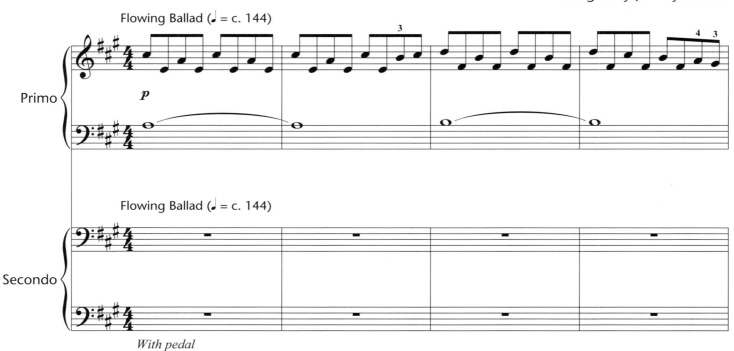

24

I Got You
(I Feel Good)

Words and Music by
James Brown
Arranged by Jeremy Siskind

31

I Want You Back

Words and Music by Freddie Perren,
Alphonso Mizell, Berry Gordy Jr.
and Deke Richards
Arranged by Jeremy Siskind

L.H. 8vb throughout

33

Isn't She Lovely

Words and Music by
Stevie Wonder
Arranged by Jeremy Siskind

Just the Way You Are

Words and Music by Bruno Mars,
Ari Levine, Philip Lawrence,
Khari Cain and Khalil Walton
Arranged by Jeremy Siskind

45

Respect

Words and Music by
Otis Redding
Arranged by Jeremy Siskind

POPULAR SONGS

HAL LEONARD STUDENT PIANO LIBRARY

The **Hal Leonard Student Piano Library** has great songs, and you will find all your favorites here: Disney classics, Broadway and movie favorites, and today's top hits. These graded collections are skillfully and imaginatively arranged for students and pianists at every level, from elementary solos with teacher accompaniments to sophisticated piano solos for the advancing pianist.

Adele
arr. Mona Rejino
00159590 Correlates with HLSPL Level 5...........$12.99

The Beatles
arr. Eugénie Rocherolle
00296649 Correlates with HLSPL Level 5 ....$10.99

Irving Berlin Piano Duos
arr. Don Heitler and Jim Lyke
00296838 Correlates with HLSPL Level 5...........$14.99

Broadway Hits
arr. Carol Klose
00296650 Correlates with HLSPL Levels 4/5........$8.99

Chart Hits
arr. Mona Rejino
00296710 Correlates with HLSPL Level 5.............$8.99

Christmas Cheer
arr. Phillip Keveren
00296616 Correlates with HLSPL Level 4.............$6.95

Classic Christmas Favorites
arr. Jennifer & Mike Watts
00129582 Correlates with HLSPL Level 5.............$9.99

Christmas Time Is Here
arr. Eugénie Rocherolle
00296614 Correlates with HLSPL Level 5.............$8.99

Classic Joplin Rags
arr. Fred Kern
00296743 Correlates with HLSPL Level 5.............$9.99

**Classical Pop –
Lady Gaga Fugue & Other Pop Hits**
arr. Giovanni Dettori
00296921 Correlates with HLSPL Level 5...........$12.99

Contemporary Movie Hits
arr. by Carol Klose, Jennifer Linn and Wendy Stevens
00296780 Correlates with HLSPL Level 5.............$8.99

Contemporary Pop Hits
arr. Wendy Stevens
00296836 Correlates with HLSPL Level 3.............$8.99

Country Favorites
arr. Mona Rejino
00296861 Correlates with HLSPL Level 5.............$9.99

Current Hits
arr. Mona Rejino
00296768 Correlates with HLSPL Level 5.............$8.99

Disney Favorites
arr. Phillip Keveren
00296647 Correlates with HLSPL Levels 3/4........$9.99

Disney Film Favorites
arr. Mona Rejino
00296809 Correlates with HLSPL Level 5...........$10.99

Easy Christmas Duets
arr. Mona Rejino and Phillip Keveren
00237139 Correlates with HLSPL Level 3/4 ....$9.99

Four Hands on Broadway
arr. Fred Kern
00146177 Correlates with HLSPL Level 5...........$12.99

Jazz Hits for Piano Duet
arr. Jeremy Siskind
00143248 Correlates with HLSPL Level 5 ....$10.99

Elton John
arr. Carol Klose
00296721 Correlates with HLSPL Level 5.............$8.99

Joplin Ragtime Duets
arr. Fred Kern
00296771 Correlates with HLSPL Level 5.............$8.99

Jerome Kern Classics
arr. Eugénie Rocherolle
00296577 Correlates with HLSPL Level 5...........$12.99

Pop Hits for Piano Duet
arr. Jeremy Siskind
00224734 Correlates with HLSPL Level 5...........$10.99

Sing to the King
arr. Phillip Keveren
00296808 Correlates with HLSPL Level 5.............$8.99

Spooky Halloween Tunes
arr. Fred Kern
00121550 Correlates with HLSPL Levels 3/4........$9.99

Today's Hits
arr. Mona Rejino
00296646 Correlates with HLSPL Level 5.............$7.99

Top Hits
arr. Jennifer and Mike Watts
00296894 Correlates with HLSPL Level 5...........$10.99

Top Piano Ballads
arr. Jennifer Watts
00197926 Correlates with HLSPL Level 5...........$10.99

You Raise Me Up
arr. Deborah Brady
00296576 Correlates with HLSPL Levels 2/3........$7.95

HAL•LEONARD ®
7777 W. BLUEMOUND RD. P.O. BOX 13819 MILWAUKEE, WI 53213

Visit our website at **www.halleonard.com**

Prices, contents and availability subject to change without notice. Prices may vary outside the U.S.